Tasty Soups

By: Kevin Lynch

ClosetCooking.com

Table of Contents

Introduction

Hi! I am Kevin Lynch and I am the author of ClosetCooking.com, a food and recipe website, where I share my favourite recipes that I cook in my closet sized kitchen. I am a big fan of soups, especially in the winter where a bowl of soup warms both the body and the soul. Soups are pure comfort food and I could never turn down a bowl. In this book I share with you 25 of the tastiest soups that I have ever made! Some of these recipes come from ClosetCooking.com and others that are completely new.

Enjoy!

Kevin Lynch

Broths and Stocks

Before we get into the soups I want to take a minute to talk about broths and stocks. Most soup recipes call for a broth or a stock for the liquid base and the terms are often used interchangeably but there is a difference. The main difference between broths and stock is that a broth is made by simmering meat in water and stocks are made by simmering bones in water. Broths tend to be lighter and clearer and stocks tend to be more full bodied and flavourful. Broths and stocks can generally be used interchangeably in soups, and this is the case for all of the recipes in this book, just keep in mind that stocks are going to be stronger.

It is really easy to make both broths and stocks at home and they are a great way to use leftovers that might have been thrown away otherwise. Whenever you cook chicken or any other meat with bones, place the bones in a freezer bag and save them to make some stock. In addition to the meat or bones, broths and stocks are made with vegetables and herbs so instead of throwing out the ends of onions, leeks, carrots, celery, etc., add them to the stock freezer bag along with any leftover fresh herbs. This is particularly efficient when making soups like chicken noodle soup where you can use the full chicken to make a broth for the soup, use the meat in the soup and then turn around and use the bones and leftover bits of onions, carrots and celery to make a stock. Don't worry about any leftover broth or stock as it freezes well and you can save it until you make another soup. Although homemade broths and stocks are going to be more flavourful than store bought ones, store bough ones are definitely convenient and save time.

Chicken Broth

Prep Time: 5 minutes **Cook Time**: 1 hour
Total Time: 1 hour 5 minutes **Servings**: 6

Easy homemade chicken broth that's perfect for any soup!

ingredients

1 (3 pound) chicken
1 onion, coarsely chopped
2 carrots, coarsely chopped
2 stalks celery, coarsely chopped
2 cloves garlic, smashed
6 sprigs parsley
1 sprig thyme
1/2 teaspoon black peppercorns
2 bay leaves
1 (2-inch) piece parmesan cheese rind (optional)
water

directions

1. Place everything in a large stock pot, cover with 4 inches of water, bring to a boil, reduce the heat and simmer, covered, for 1 hour.
2. Pull the meat off of the chicken and reserve for another use.
3. Strain the solids from the broth and discard them.
4. Optionally, let the broth cool in the fridge overnight and skim off any fat before using.

Tip: When making other recipes, save any leftover celery and carrot ends, herbs and parmesan rinds in the freezer for the next time that you make chicken broth.
Tip: Save the chicken carcass to make chicken stock.
Tip: Chicken broth freezes well so you don't have to use it all when you make it.

Nutrition Facts: Calories 14, Fat 0.8g (Saturated 0.2g, Trans 0), Cholesterol 4mg, Sodium 7mg, Carbs 0.2g (Fiber 0, Sugars 0), Protein 1g

Chicken Stock

Prep Time: 5 minutes **Cook Time**: 2 hours
Total Time: 2 hours 5 minutes **Servings**: 6

Easy homemade chicken stock that is healthy, full of flavour and perfect for any soup!

ingredients
1-3 chicken carcasses
1 onion, coarsely chopped
2 carrots, coarsely chopped
2 stalks celery, coarsely chopped
2 cloves garlic, smashed
6 sprigs parsley
1 sprig thyme
1/2 teaspoon black peppercorns
2 bay leaves
1 (2-inch) piece parmesan cheese rind (optional)
water

directions
1. Place everything in a large stock pot, cover with 4 inches of water, bring to a boil, reduce the heat and simmer, covered, for 2 hours.
2. Strain the solids from the stock and discard them.
3. Optionally, let the stock cool in the fridge overnight and skim off any fat before using.

Tip: Chicken stock freezes well so you don't have to use it all when you make it.

Nutrition Facts: Calories 14, Fat 0.8g (Saturated 0.2g, Trans 0), Cholesterol 4mg, Sodium 7mg, Carbs 0.2g (Fiber 0, Sugars 0), Protein 1g

Chicken Noodle Soup

Prep Time: 10 minutes **Cook Time**: 20 minutes
Total Time: 30 minutes **Servings**: 4

A quick and easy homemade chicken noodle soup that's pure comfort food and lick your bowl clean good!

ingredients
1 tablespoon oil
1 onion, diced
2 carrots, diced
2 stalks celery, diced
4 cups chicken broth (or chicken stock)
2 cups cooked chicken, sliced
1 teaspoon poultry seasoning
2 cups egg noodles (gluten-free for gluten-free)
1/2 lemon, juice (optional)
salt and pepper to taste
1 handful parsley, chopped

directions
1. Heat the oil in a large stock pot over medium-high heat, add the onion, carrot and celery and cook until tender, about 8-10 minutes.
2. Add the chicken broth, chicken and poultry seasoning, bring to a boil, reduce the heat and simmer for 5 minutes.
3. Add the noodles and simmer until just tender, about 5 minutes.
4. Season with salt and pepper to taste and mix in the parsley.

Option: Pulse half of the onion, carrot and celery in a food processor until they are in grainy bits, do the first step with only the pureed veggies, cooking until they get nice and caramelized before deglazing the pan with the chicken broth and adding the remaining veggies. This way the pureed vegetables get amazingly caramelized and add a ton of flavour and the remaining veggies keep more of their texture because they are cooked less.
Option: Replace the oil with bacon grease.
Option: Add 1 tablespoon white miso in the final step.
Option: Mix in 1/4 cup finely grated parmigiano reggiano (parmesan) in the last step.
Slow Cooker: Optionally implement step 1, place everything except the noodles, parmesan and parsley in the slow cooker and cook on low for 6-10 hours or high for 2-4 hours before adding the noodles, cooking on high until tender, about 10 minutes, and mixing in the parmesan and parsley. Another option is to use whole chicken breasts or thighs, placing them in the slow cooker with everything and pulling them out, shredding and returning to the soup when it is done cooking.

Nutrition Facts: Calories 147, Fat 3.7g (Saturated 0.6g, Trans 0), Cholesterol 38mg, Sodium 144mg, Carbs 16.2g (Fiber 2g, Sugars 2.1g), Protein 12g

Roasted Cauliflower and Aged White Cheddar Soup

Prep Time: 10 minutes **Cook Time**: 50 minutes
Total Time: 1 hour **Servings**: 4

A creamy white cheddar cheese cauliflower soup with a hint of thyme.

ingredients

1 small head cauliflower, cut into florets
2 tablespoons oil
salt and pepper to taste
1 tablespoon oil
1 medium onion, diced
2 cloves garlic, chopped
1 teaspoon thyme, chopped
4 cups vegetable broth (or chicken broth)
1 1/2 cups aged white cheddar, shredded
1 cup cream (or milk)
salt and pepper to taste

directions

1. Toss the cauliflower florets in the oil along with the salt and pepper, arrange them in a single layer on a large baking sheet and roast in a preheated 400F/200C oven until lightly golden brown, about 20-30 minutes, flipping halfway through.
2. Heat the oil in a large saucepan over medium heat, add the onion and cook until tender, about 5-7 minutes.
3. Add the garlic and thyme and cook until fragrant, about a minute.
4. Add the broth, deglaze the pan, add the cauliflower, bring to a boil, reduce the heat and simmer, covered, for 20 minutes.
5. Puree the soup until it reaches your desired consistency with a stick blender, or in a food processor, or in a blender.
6. Mix in the cheese, let it melt, without bringing it to boil again.
7. Mix in the cream, season with salt and pepper and remove from heat.

Slow Cooker: Implement step 1, optionally implement steps 2 and 3, place everything except the cheese and milk in the slow cooker and cook on low for 6-10 hours or high for 2-4 hours before adding the cheese and milk and cooking until the cheese has melted.

Note: The amount of broth that you are going to need will depend on how large your head of cauliflower is and how thick or thin you want the soup to be.

Nutrition Facts: Calories 214, Fat 11.2g (Saturated 3.5g, Trans 0), Cholesterol 14mg, Sodium 372mg, Carbs 13.1g (Fiber 3.2g, Sugars 6.6g), Protein 16.2g

Buffalo Chicken Chowder

Prep Time: 10 minutes **Cook Time**: 25 minutes
Total Time: 35 minutes **Servings**: 4

A hearty and creamy chowder with all of the
flavours of buffalo chicken wings!

ingredients

2 tablespoons butter
1 onion, diced
2 carrots, diced
2 stalks celery, diced
2 cloves garlic, chopped
1/4 cup flour (rice flour for gluten-free)
4 cups chicken broth (or chicken stock)
1 pound cooked chicken, diced or shredded
1/4 cup hot sauce (such as Franks Red Hot)
1 large yukon gold (or other boiling potato), peeled and cut into bite sized pieces
salt and pepper to taste
1 cup heavy cream (or milk)
1/4 cup blue cheese, crumbled (optional)

directions

1. Melt the butter in a large saucepan over medium-high heat, add the onion, carrots and celery
   and cook until tender, about 8-10 minutes.
2. Add the garlic and cook until fragrant, about a minute.
3. Mix in the flour and let it cook for 2-3 minutes.
4. Add the chicken broth, chicken, hot sauce and potatoes, bring to a boil, reduce the heat and
   simmer until the potatoes are tender, about 10-15 minutes.
5. Season with salt and pepper, mix in the cream and blue cheese and remove from heat when the
   cheese has melted.

Slow Cooker: Implement steps 1-3, place everything except the cream and cheese in the slow cooker and
cook on low for 6-10 hours or high for 2-4 hours before adding the cream and cheese.
Slow Cooker: Melt the butter in a large saucepan over medium heat, add the flour, cook for 2-3 minutes,
add the broth, place everything except the cream and cheese in the slow cooker and cook on low for 6-
10 hours or high for 2-4 hours before adding the cream and cheese.
Slow Cooker: Instead of using cooked chicken, used uncooked boneless, skinless chicken breasts or
thighs, place them in the slow cooker with everything else and when done cooking, remove them, dice
or shred them and return them to the soup.
Note: Hot sauces vary in heat, use as much of your hot sauce as required to get the level of heat that you
like!

Nutrition Facts: Calories 576, Fat 38g (Saturated 21g, Trans 0), Cholesterol 188mg, Sodium 619mg,
Carbs 24g (Fiber 3g, Sugars 5g), Protein 34g

Lasagna Soup

Prep Time: 10 minutes **Cook Time**: 40 minutes
Total Time: 50 minutes **Servings**: 4

Lasagna is made with a tomato based meat sauce layered with pasta and cheese and this soup has it all from the tasty Italian sausage and tomatoes to the pasta and it is topped off with a dollop of cheesy goodness that will warm your heart.

ingredients

1 tablespoon oil
1 pound Italian sausage, casings removed
1 onion, diced
2 cloves garlic, chopped
1/2 teaspoon red pepper flakes (optional)
1/2 teaspoon ground fennel seeds (optional)
2 tablespoons tomato paste
4 cups chicken broth (or chicken stock)
1 (28 ounce) can diced tomatoes
1 teaspoon oregano
1 bay leaf
1/2 pound pasta (gluten-free for gluten-free)
salt and pepper to taste
4 ounces ricotta
1/4 cup parmigiano reggiano (parmesan cheese), grated
1 cup mozzarella cheese, shredded
1 handful basil, chopped

directions

1. Heat the oil in a large saucepan over medium heat, add the sausage and cook until lightly browned, about 10 minutes, breaking it apart as it cooks, and set aside, reserving the remaining oil and grease.
2. Add the onion and cook until tender, about 5-7 minutes.
3. Add the garlic, red pepper flakes, fennel, and tomato paste, and cook until fragrant, about a minute.
4. Add the chicken broth, tomatoes, sausage, oregano, and bay leaf, bring to a boil, reduce the heat and simmer for 10 minutes.
5. Add the pasta and cook until al-dente, about 7 minutes and remove from heat.
6. Season with salt and pepper to taste.
7. Mix the ricotta, parmesan and mozzarella and serve the soup garnished with a tablespoon of the mixture along with the basil.

Slow Cooker: Implement step 1, optionally implement steps 2 and 3, place everything except the pasta, the cheeses and basil, in the slow cooker and cook on low for 6-10 hours or high for 2-4 hours before adding the pasta and cooking on high until the pasta is cooked, about 10 minutes.

Nutrition Facts: Calories 779, Fat 61g (Saturated 26g, Trans 0), Cholesterol 157mg, Sodium 1548mg, Carbs 58g (Fiber 6g, Sugars 9g), Protein 48g

Ale and Cheddar Soup

Prep Time: 10 minutes **Cook Time**: 40 minutes
Total Time: 50 minutes **Servings**: 4

A heavenly ale and melted cheddar cheese soup seasoned with smoky bacon and spicy jalapenos that's pure comfort in a bowl!

ingredients

1/2 pound bacon, cut into 1 inch slices
1 onion, diced
2 stalks celery, diced
2 jalapeno peppers, diced
2 cloves garlic, chopped
1 teaspoon thyme, chopped
2 tablespoons butter
1/4 cup flour (rice flour for gluten-free)
2 cups chicken broth (or vegetable broth)
2 cups ale (gluten-free for gluten-free) (or more broth)
1 teaspoon dijon mustard
1 tablespoon worcestershire sauce
1/2 cup heavy cream (or milk)
2 cups cheddar cheese, shredded
cayenne, salt and pepper to taste

directions

1. Cook the bacon in a large saucepan over medium heat and set aside on paper towels to drain, reserving 2 tablespoons of the grease in the pan.
2. Add the onion, celery and jalapeno and cook until tender, about 10 minutes.
3. Add the garlic and thyme and cook until fragrant, about a minute.
4. Add the butter, let it melt and start bubbling, before sprinkling on the flour and letting it cook until it starts to turn golden brown, about 2-3 minutes.
5. Add the broth, and ale, and deglaze the pan before adding the bacon and then let cook for 10 minutes.
6. Add the mustard, Worcestershire sauce, cream, and cheese, and cook, until the cheese has melted, without bringing it back to a boil.
7. Season with cayenne, salt and pepper to taste and enjoy.

Slow Cooker: Implement step 1, optionally implement steps 2 and 3, implement step 4, place everything except the cream and cheese in the slow cooker and cook on low for 6-10 hours or high for 2-4 hours before adding the cream and cheese and letting the cheese melt.
Option: Omit the bacon and use 2 tablespoons of butter or oil instead.

Nutrition Facts: Calories 658, Fat 61g (Saturated 29g, Trans 0.8g), Cholesterol 158mg, Sodium 1167mg, Carbs 22g (Fiber 1g, Sugars 7g), Protein 28g

Spinach, White Bean and Turkey Sausage Soup

Prep Time: 5 minutes **Cook Time**: 25 minutes
Total Time: 30 minutes **Servings**: 4

A quick and easy soup with Italian turkey sausage, white beans and spinach, that's full of flavour, nice and healthy.

ingredients

1 tablespoon olive oil
1 pound Italian turkey sausage, casings removed
2 cloves garlic, chopped
1 pinch red pepper flakes (optional)
4 cups chicken broth (or chicken stock)
1 (14.5 ounce) can cannellini beans, drained and rinsed
1 teaspoon oregano
1 bunch spinach (or kale or swiss chard), coarsely chopped
1/4 cup parmigiano reggiano (parmesan cheese), grated
1 tablespoon lemon juice
salt and pepper to taste

directions

1. Heat the oil in a large saucepan over medium-high heat, add the sausage and cook, breaking it apart as it cooks.
2. Add garlic and red chili pepper flakes and cook until fragrant, about a minute.
3. Add the broth, beans, and oregano, bring to a boil, reduce the heat and simmer for 10 minutes, before turning off the heat
4. Add the spinach and parmesan, and let the spinach wilt and the cheese melt, about 2-3 minutes.
5. Add the lemon juice and season with salt, pepper to taste.

Nutrition Facts: Calories 424, Fat 15g (Saturated 3g, Trans 0.3g), Cholesterol 92mg, Sodium 1049mg, Carbs 33g (Fiber 6g, Sugars 4g), Protein 36g

Reuben Soup

Prep Time: 10 minutes **Cook Time**: 30 minutes
Total Time: 40 minutes **Servings**: 4

A hearty soup with all of the flavours of a reuben
sandwich served French onion soup style topped
with dark rye and melted swiss.

ingredients
3 tablespoons butter
1 onion, diced
2 cloves garlic, chopped
1/2 teaspoon red pepper flakes (optional)
1/4 cup flour (or rice flour for gluten-free)
4 cups chicken broth (or chicken stock)
1 cup cooked corned beef, shredded or cut into bite sized pieces
1 cup sauerkraut, drained, coarsely chopped
2 medium Yukon Gold potatoes, peeled and cut into bite sized pieces
1 tablespoon Worcestershire sauce
1 teaspoon (corned beef) pickling spices
1/4 teaspoon caraway seeds
1/2 cup heavy cream (or milk)
4 slices dark rye, lightly toasted (gluten-free for gluten-free)
2 cups swiss cheese, shredded

directions
1. Melt the butter in a large saucepan over medium heat, add the onion and cook until tender,
   about 5-7 minutes.
2. Add the garlic and red pepper flakes and cook until fragrant, about 1 minute.
3. Mix in the flour and cook for 2-3 minutes.
4. Add the broth, deglaze the pan, add the corned beef, sauerkraut, potatoes, Worcestershire
   sauce, pickling spices, and caraway seeds, bring to a boil, reduce the heat and simmer until the
   potatoes are tender, about 10-15 minutes.
5. Add the cream, season with salt and pepper.
6. Divide between 4 oven-safe bowls, top with the rye and swiss and broil until the cheese melts,
   about 1-3 minutes.

Slow Cooker: Implement step 1, optionally implement steps 2 and 3, place everything except the cream,
bread and cheese in the slow cooker and cook on low for 6-10 hours or high for 2-4 hours before adding
the cream and optionally implementing step 6.

Nutrition Facts: Calories 635, Fat 39g (Saturated 23g, Trans 0.3g), Cholesterol 128mg, Sodium 851mg,
Carbs 42g (Fiber 4g, Sugars 8g), Protein 27g

Chicken Pot Pie Soup

Prep Time: 10 minutes **Cook Time**: 30 minutes
Total Time: 40 minutes **Servings**: 4

All of the flavours of a chicken pot pie served as a soup topped with crispy, flaky, golden brown puff pastry 'crust'.

ingredients
2 tablespoon butter
1 onion, diced
2 carrots, diced
2 stalks celery, diced
2 cloves garlic, chopped
1/4 cup flour (rice flour for gluten-free)
4 cups chicken broth (or chicken stock)
2 cups potatoes, cut into small pieces
1 teaspoon poultry seasoning
2 cups cooked chicken, cut into small pieces
1/2 cup corn
1/2 cup peas
1/2 cup heavy cream (or milk)
salt and pepper to taste
1 sheet puff pastry, cut into circles that will fit over
   your bowls (gluten-free for gluten-free)

directions
1. Melt the butter in a large saucepan over medium heat, add the onion, carrots, celery and cook until tender, about 8-10 minutes.
2. Add the garlic and cook until fragrant, about a minute.
3. Mix in the flour and cook for 2-3 minutes.
4. Add the chicken broth, potatoes, poultry seasoning and chicken, bring to a boil, reduce the heat and simmer until the potatoes are tender, about 10-15 minutes.
5. Turn off the heat, and add the corn, peas, and cream.
6. Season with salt and pepper.
7. Meanwhile, bake the puff pastry in a preheated 350F oven on a greased baking sheet until golden brown, about 8-10 minutes.
8. Serve the soup in bowls topped with the puff pastry.

Option: Add 1 tablespoon white miso just before seasoning with salt and pepper.
Option: Add 1/4 cup parmesan before seasoning with salt and pepper.

Nutrition Facts: Calories 526, Fat 26g (Saturated 13g, Trans 0), Cholesterol 113mg, Sodium 542mg, Carbs 43g (Fiber 5g, Sugars 9g), Protein 28g

Creamy Cabbage and Double Smoked Bacon Soup

Prep Time: 10 minutes **Cook Time**: 45 minutes
Total Time: 55 minutes **Servings**: 4

A hearty and creamy soup with double smoked bacon, sausage and cabbage that's just packed with flavour.

ingredients

1 tablespoon olive oil
1/2 pound Italian sausage, casing removed
1/2 pound double smoked bacon, cut into 1 inch pieces
1 onion, diced
2 carrots, diced
2 stalks celery, diced
2 cloves garlic, chopped
1 (14.5 ounce) can cannellini beans, drained and rinsed
4 cups ham broth (or chicken broth)
1/2 small head cabbage, thinly sliced
1 teaspoon oregano
1/4 cup heavy cream
salt and pepper to taste
2 tablespoons parsley, chopped

directions

1. Heat the oil in a large saucepan over medium-high heat, add the sausage, and cook until cooked, about 8-10 minutes, breaking it up as you go and set it aside.
2. Add the bacon to the pan and cook until cooked, about 8-10 minutes, and set it aside, reserving 1 tablespoon of grease in the pan
3. Add the onion, carrot and celery and cook until tender, about 8-10 minutes.
4. Add the garlic and cook until fragrant, about a minute.
5. Puree half of the beans in a food processor with some of the chicken stock.
6. Add the chicken stock, sausage, bacon, beans, pureed beans, cabbage, and oregano, and bring to a boil, reduce the heat and simmer until the cabbage is tender, about 10-15 minutes.
7. Season with salt and pepper, mix in the cream and parsley and remove from heat.

Slow Cooker: Implement steps 1 and 2, optionally implement steps 2 and 3, place everything except the cream and parsley in the slow cooker and cook on low for 6-10 hours or high for 2-4 hours before adding the cream and parsley.
Option: Serve garnished with grainy mustard.

Nutrition Facts: Calories 689, Fat 49g (Saturated 17g, Trans 0), Cholesterol 100mg, Sodium 856mg, Carbs 36g (Fiber 9g, Sugars 7g), Protein 25g

Beer Mac n Cheese Soup

Prep Time: 10 minutes **Cook Time**: 35 minutes
Total Time: 45 minutes **Servings**: 4

All of the flavours of mac n cheese in the form of a
hot bowl of soup!

ingredients

6 strips bacon, cut into 1 inch slices (optional)
1 onion, diced
2 carrots, diced
2 stalks celery, diced
1 jalapeno pepper, diced
2 cloves garlic, chopped
1/4 cup flour (rice flour for gluten-free)
4 cups chicken broth (or vegetable broth)
2 cups beer (gluten-free for gluten-free)
1 pinch nutmeg (optional)
1 teaspoon dijon mustard
1 tablespoon worcestershire sauce
1 cup elbow macaroni (gluten-free for gluten-free)
1/2 cup heavy cream (or milk)
3 cups cheddar cheese, shredded
cayenne, salt and pepper to taste

directions

1. Cook the bacon in a pan over medium heat and set aside on paper towels to drain, reserving 4
   tablespoons of the grease in the pan.
2. Add the onion, carrot, celery and jalapeno and cook until tender, about 8-10 minutes.
3. Add the garlic and cook until fragrant, about a minute.
4. Mix in the flour and let it cook for 2-3 minutes.
5. Add the broth, beer, nutmeg, mustard, worcestershire sauce, bacon and macaroni and let cook
   until the macaroni is al-dente, about 7 minutes.
6. Add the cream and cheese and cook until the cheese has melted without bringing it back to a
   boil.
7. Season with cayenne, salt and pepper to taste.

Slow Cooker: Implement step 1, optionally implement steps 2-3 or skip ahead and implement step 4,
place everything except the pasta, cream and cheese in the slow cooker and cook on low for 6-10 hours
or high for 2-4 hours before adding the pasta, cooking on high until al-dente, about 20-30 minutes, and
mixing in the cream and cheese until the cheese melts.
Option: Omit bacon and use 4 tablespoons of butter or oil.
Option: Add broccoli florets!

Nutrition Facts: Calories 870, Fat 57g (Saturated 29g, Trans 1g), Cholesterol 155mg, Sodium 948mg,
Carbs 42g (Fiber 2g, Sugars 5g), Protein 32g

Pretzel Rolls

Prep Time: 10 minutes **Rise Time**: 2 hours
Cook Time: 25 minutes **Total Time**: 2 hours 35 minutes
Servings: 8

Quick and easy pretzel rolls for any occasion.

ingredients
2 3/4 cups bread flour
1 envelope quick-rising yeast
1 teaspoon salt
1 teaspoon sugar
1 teaspoon celery seeds
1 cup plus 2 tablespoons hot water (125°F to 130°F)
8 cups water
1/4 cup baking soda
2 tablespoons sugar
1 egg white, beaten to blend (glaze)
Coarse salt

directions
1. Mix the bread flour, yeast, salt, sugar and celery seeds in a food processor and gradually pour in the hot water until it forms an elastic dough.
2. Place the dough in a greased bowl and cover until it has doubled in size, about 1-2 hours.
3. Punch the dough down, form it into 8 balls cutting an X on the top of each with a serrated knife, cover and let rise until doubled in size, about 1-2 hours.
4. Bring the water to a boil, add the baking soda and sugar and cook the rolls for 30 seconds per side.
5. Place the rolls on a greased baking sheet, brush the tops with the egg, sprinkle on some salt and bake in a preheated 375F/190C oven until golden brown, about 25 minutes.

Nutrition Facts: Calories 189, Fat 0.9g (Saturated 0.1g, Trans 0), Cholesterol 0, Sodium 1905mg, Carbs 38g (Fiber 1g, Sugars 3g), Protein 6g

Chicken Enchilada Soup

Prep Time: 10 minutes **Cook Time**: 20 minutes
Total Time: 30 minutes **Servings**: 4

A chicken soup with all of the flavours of chicken enchiladas that is both hearty and healthy!

ingredients

1 tablespoon oil
1 onion, diced
1/2 red bell pepper, diced
2 cloves garlic, chopped
1 teaspoon ground cumin
1 teaspoon chipotle chili powder (or to taste)
1/2 teaspoon smoked paprika
4 cups chicken broth (or chicken stock)
1 (10 ounce) can enchilada sauce
1 (14.5 ounce) can diced tomatoes
1 (14.5 ounce) can black beans, drained and rinsed
1/2 teaspoon oregano
1 pound boneless and skinless chicken breasts or
  thighs
1 cup corn
1 tablespoon lime juice
cayenne, salt and pepper to taste
2 tablespoons cilantro, chopped

directions

1. Heat the oil in a large saucepan over medium heat, add the onion and red bell pepper and cook until tender, about 8-10 minutes.
2. Add the garlic, cumin, chipotle chili powder, and smoked paprika and cook until fragrant, about a minute.
3. Add the broth, enchilada sauce, diced tomatoes, black beans, oregano and chicken, bring to a boil, reduce the heat and simmer for 10-15 minutes.
4. Add the corn and simmer for another 5 minutes, before adding the lime juice.
5. Season with cayenne, salt, and pepper to taste, mix in the cilantro, and remove from heat.

Option: Use cooked chicken and cut simmer time down to 10 minutes!
Option: Serve garnished with your favourite taco topping such as avocado, sour cream, cheese and/or tortilla chips.

Nutrition Facts: Calories 453, Fat 10g (Saturated 1g, Trans 0), Cholesterol 89mg, Sodium 1194mg, Carbs 48g (Fiber 12g, Sugars 15g), Protein 42g

Bacon Double Cheeseburger Soup

Prep Time: 10 minutes **Cook Time**: 50 minutes
Total Time: 1 hour **Servings**: 4

A tasty and hearty soup with all of the flavours of a bacon double cheeseburgers!

ingredients

1 pound ground beef
8 slices bacon, cut into one inch pieces
1 onion, diced
2 carrots, diced
2 stalks celery, diced
1 jalapeno, seeded and finely diced (optional)
2 cloves garlic, chopped
1/4 cup flour (rice flour for gluten-free)
2 cups beef broth
2 cups beer (gluten-free for gluten-free) (or more broth)
1 large yukon gold (or other boiling potato), peeled and cut into bite sized pieces
2 tablespoons ketchup
1 teaspoon mustard
1 tablespoon worcestershire sauce
1 (14.5 ounce) can diced tomatoes
2 cups lettuce, shredded
1 cup milk (or cream)
1 cup cheddar cheese, shredded
1 cup mozzarella cheese, shredded
cayenne, salt and pepper to taste
2 hamburger buns, cut into 1 inch cubes (gluten-free or omit for gluten-free)
1 tablespoon bacon grease (or oil)
salt and pepper to taste

directions

1. Cook the ground beef in a large saucepan over medium heat, about 8-10 minutes, and set aside.
2. Cook the bacon in the pan, about 5-7 minutes, and set aside on paper towels, reserving about 4 tablespoons of the grease in the pan.
3. Add the onions, carrots, celery and jalapeno and cook until tender, about 10-15 minutes.
4. Add the garlic and cook until fragrant, about a minute
5. Mix in the flour and let it cook for 2-3 minutes.
6. Add the broth, beer, bacon, beef, potato, ketchup, mustard, worcestershire sauce and tomatoes, bring to a boil, reduce the heat and simmer until the potatoes are tender, about 10-15 minutes.
7. Add the lettuce, milk and cheese and cook until the cheese has melted, without bringing it back to a boil.
8. Season with cayenne, salt and pepper to taste!
9. While the soup is cooking, toss the bun cubes in bacon grease, salt, and pepper, and bake in a preheated 400F/200C oven until lightly golden brown, about 10 minutes, turning half way

through.

10. Serve garnished with the croutons!

Slow Cooker: Implement step 1 and 2, optionally implement steps 3 and 4, implement step 5, place everything except the milk, cheese and buns in the slow cooker and cook on low for 6-10 hours or high for 2-4 hours before adding the milk and cheese and continuing to cook until the cheese melts and optionally implementing step 9.

Option: Garnish with your favourite burger toppings such add: shredded cheese, diced pickles, shredded lettuce, diced tomatoes, etc.

Nutrition Facts: Calories 1085, Fat 68g (Saturated 27g, Trans 1g), Cholesterol 175mg, Sodium 1378mg, Carbs 53g (Fiber 5g, Sugars 14g), Protein 51g

Creamy Tomato, Basil and Parmesan Soup

Prep Time: 10 minutes **Cook Time**: 20 minutes
Total Time: 30 minutes **Servings**: 4

A creamy tomato and parmesan soup that is just brimming with vegetables and flavour.

ingredients
3 tablespoons butter
1 onion, diced
2 carrots, diced
2 stalks celery, diced
2 cloves garlic, chopped
2 tablespoons tomato paste
1/4 cup flour (rice flour for gluten-free)
4 cups chicken broth (or vegetable broth)
1 (28 ounce) can diced tomatoes
1 teaspoon dried oregano
1 teaspoon dried basil
1/2 cup heavy cream (or milk)
1/2 cup parmigiano reggiano (parmesan cheese), grated
salt and pepper to taste
1/4 cup fresh basil, thinly sliced (optional)

directions
1. Melt the butter in a large saucepan over medium heat, add the onions, carrots, and celery, and cook until tender, about 8-10 minutes.
2. Add the garlic and tomato paste and cook until fragrant, about a minute.
3. Mix in the flour and let it cook for 2-3 minutes.
4. Add the chicken broth, tomatoes, oregano, and basil, deglaze the pan, bring to a boil, reduce the heat and simmer for 10 minutes.
5. Add the cream, and parmesan, and season with salt and pepper to taste before serving garnished with fresh basil.

Nutrition Facts: Calories 527, Fat 41g (Saturated 25g, Trans 0.3g), Cholesterol 129mg, Sodium 684mg, Carbs 24g (Fiber 6g, Sugars 11g), Protein 18g

French Onion Soup

Prep Time: 15 minutes **Cook Time**: 3 hours 30 minutes
Total Time: 3 hours 45 minutes **Servings**: 4

A decadent French onion soup with a beautiful depth of flavour that's topped with toast and melted cheese.

ingredients
1/4 cup butter
4 pounds onions, sliced
2 cloves garlic, chopped
1 teaspoon thyme, chopped
1/4 cup flour (rice flour for gluten-free)
1 cup red wine (or broth)
3 cups beef broth or vegetable broth
2 bay leaves
salt and pepper to taste
4 1/2 inch thick slices of day old bread, toasted
   (gluten-free or omit for gluten-free)
1 cup gruyere cheese (or swiss), shredded
1/4 cup parmigiano reggiano (parmesan cheese),
   grated

directions
1. Melt the butter in a large saucepan over medium-low heat, add the onions and cook slowly, with the lid on, until golden brown and caramelized, about 2-3 hours, stirring every 15 minutes.
2. Raise the heat to medium, add the garlic and thyme and cook until fragrant, about a minute.
3. Mix in the flour and let it cook for 2-3 minutes.
4. Add the wine and deglaze the pan.
5. Add the broth and bay leaves, bring to a boil, reduce the heat and simmer, covered, for 30 minutes, before removing bay leaves.
6. Ladle the soup into 4 oven-proof bowls, place on a baking sheet and top with the sliced bread and cheese.
7. Broil until cheese melts, about 1-3 minutes.

Option: Add 1 tablespoon balsamic vinegar.
Option: Add 1 tablespoon soy sauce.

Nutrition Facts: Calories 626, Fat 26g (Saturated 15g, Trans 0.3g), Cholesterol 73mg, Sodium 578mg, Carbs 67g (Fiber 9g, Sugars 21g), Protein 22g

Shrimp and Roasted Corn Chowder

Prep Time: 15 minutes **Cook Time**: 55 minutes
Total Time: 1 hour 10 minutes **Servings**: 4

A creamy and smoky shrimp and roast corn chowder; a perfect way to enjoy fresh corn from the cob.

ingredients

4 ears corn, kernels cut from the cobs, cobs reserved
1/2 pound shrimp peeled and deveined, shells reserved
4 cups chicken broth (or shrimp stock)
4 slices smoked bacon, cut into one inch pieces
1 onion, diced
2 stalks celery, diced
1/2 red bell pepper, diced
2 cloves garlic, chopped
1 teaspoon thyme, chopped
2 teaspoons smoked paprika
1/4 cup flour (or rice flour for gluten-free)
1 large stewing potato (such as a red potato or white potato), cut into bite sized pieces
1/2 cup heavy cream (or milk)
1 tablespoon fish sauce (optional)
cayenne, salt and pepper to taste

directions

1. Bring the broth, corn cobs, and shrimp shells to a boil, reduce the heat and simmer, covered, until the liquid becomes a little cloudy, about 20-30 minutes, strain and discard the solids and set the broth aside. (This step is optional but adds a ton of flavour to the chowder.)
2. Meanwhile, cook the bacon in a large saucepan over medium heat and set aside on paper towels to drain.
3. Raise the heat to medium-high, add the corn and let it sit in place until it chars a bit, about 8 minutes, mix it, repeat and set aside.
4. Reduce the heat down to medium, add the onion, celery and pepper and cook until tender, about 7-10 minutes.
5. Add the garlic, thyme and paprika and cook until fragrant, about a minute.
6. Sprinkle on the flour and cook for 2-3 minutes.
7. Add the broth, corn, and potato and simmer until the potato is tender, about 10-15 minutes.
8. Add the cream and shrimp and simmer until the shrimp is cooked, about 2-3 minutes.
9. Add the fish sauce and season with cayenne, salt and pepper to taste.

Slow Cooker: Optionally implement step 1, implement step 2, optionally implement steps 3-5, implement step 6, place everything except the cream in the slow cooker and cook on low for 6-10 hours or high for 2-4 hours before adding the cream.

Nutrition Facts: Calories 456, Fat 24g (Saturated 11g, Trans 0), Cholesterol 151mg, Sodium 316mg, Carbs 41g (Fiber 4g, Sugars 10g), Protein 21g

Pizza Soup

Prep Time: *10 minutes* **Cook Time**: *55 minutes*
Total Time: *1 hour 5 minutes* **Servings**: *4*

All of the flavours of a pepperoni, sausage, bacon, mushroom, and green pepper pizza in soup form that's served French onion soup style topped with toast, melted cheese and even more pizza toppings.

ingredients

1/2 pound bacon, cut into 1 inch pieces
1/2 pound Italian sausage, casings removed
4 ounces pepperoni, quartered
1 onion, diced
1 green pepper, diced
8 ounces mushrooms, sliced
2 cloves garlic, chopped
2 tablespoon tomato paste
1 (28 ounce) can diced tomatoes
3 cups chicken broth
1 teaspoon oregano
salt and pepper to taste
4 slices bread, toasted (optional)
2 cups mozzarella cheese, shredded
extra pizza topping to taste (optional)
1 tablespoon basil, julienned (optional)

directions

1. Cook the bacon in a large saucepan over medium heat, about 8-10 minutes and set aside.
2. Cook the sausage, about 8-10 minutes and set aside.
3. Cook the pepperoni, about 2-4 minutes and set aside
4. Drain all but 1 tablespoon of the grease, add the onion, green pepper, and mushrooms, and cook until tender, about 10-15 minutes
5. Add the garlic and tomato paste, and cook until fragrant, about a minute.
6. Add the tomatoes, broth, oregano, sausage, bacon, pepperoni, bring to a boil, reduce the heat and let simmer for 15 minutes.
7. Season with salt and pepper.
8. Divide the soup between 4 oven safe bowls, top with the toast, cheese and pizza toppings and broil until the cheese has melted.
9. Garnish with the basil and enjoy!

Nutrition Facts: Calories 788, Fat 81g (Saturated 30g, Trans 1g), Cholesterol 189mg, Sodium 2631mg, Carbs 37g (Fiber 6g, Sugars 14g), Protein 51g

Curried Red Lentil Soup with Chickpeas and Quinoa

Prep Time: 15 minutes **Cook Time**: 35 minutes
Total Time: 50 minutes **Servings**: 6

A healthy and hearty lentil, chickpea and quinoa soup seasoned with curry flavours.

ingredients

1 tablespoon oil
1 onion, diced
2 carrots, diced
2 stalks celery, diced
1 tablespoon garlic, chopped
1 tablespoon ginger, chopped
1 tablespoon curry powder (or 1 tablespoon garam masala + 1 teaspoon turmeric)
1 cup dry red lentils
1/3 cup quinoa
4 cups chicken broth (or vegetable broth)
1 (28 ounce) can diced tomatoes
1 (14.5 ounce) can chickpeas, rinsed and drained
1 tablespoon chili sauce (such as sambal oelek) (or to taste)
2 tablespoons cilantro, chopped
salt and pepper to taste

directions

1. Heat the oil in a pan over medium heat, add the onions, carrots, and celery, and cook until tender, about 10-15 minutes.
2. Add the garlic, ginger, and curry powder, and cook until fragrant, about a minute.
3. Add the lentils, quinoa, broth, tomatoes, chickpeas, and chili sauce, bring to a boil, reduce the heat and simmer until the lentils and quinoa are tender, about 10-15 minutes.
4. Add the cilantro and season with salt and pepper to taste.

Option: Serve garnished with plain yogurt or sour cream!

Nutrition Facts: Calories 322, Fat 6.4g (Saturated 1g, Trans 0), Cholesterol 0mg, Sodium 435mg, Carbs 48g (Fiber 16.4g, Sugars 6.8g), Protein 19g

Loaded Baked Potato Soup

Prep Time: 10 minutes **Cook Time**: 1 hour 35 minutes
Total Time: 1 hour 45 minutes **Servings**: 4

All of the flavours of fully loaded baked potatoes in
the form of a comforting soup with bacon, cheese,
sour cream and green onions that's served topped
with crispy fried potato skins!

ingredients

1 1/2 pound russet potatoes, scrubbed, dried
1/2 pound bacon, cut into 1 inch pieces
2 leeks (the whites and light greens), thinly sliced
    (or 1 large onion), diced
2 cloves garlic, chopped
1/4 cup flour (or rice flour for gluten-free)
4 cup chicken broth (or chicken stock)
1 tablespoon oil
1 tablespoon butter
3 cups cheddar cheese, shredded
4 green onions, sliced
1 cup sour cream
salt and pepper to taste

directions

1. Prick the potatoes a few times with a fork and
bake in a preheated 400F oven until tender, about an hour.
2. Let the potatoes cool, scoop flesh from the skins, roughly chop the flesh, cut the skins into bite-sized pieces and set both aside.
3. Cook the bacon in a large saucepan over medium heat until crispy, about 5-7 minutes and set aside, reserving the grease in the pan.
4. Add the leeks and cook until tender, about 3-5 minutes.
5. Add the garlic and cook until fragrant, about a minute.
6. Mix in the flour and let it cook for 2-3 minutes.
7. Add the broth and the flesh of the potatoes, bring to a boil, reduce the heat and simmer for 15 minutes.
8. Meanwhile, heat the oil and butter in a pan over medium-high heat.
9. Add the potato skins to the pan, fry until crispy, about 5-7 minutes and set them on paper towels to drain.
10. Meanwhile, mix half of the bacon, 2 cups of the cheese, 2/3 of the green onions and 2/3 of the sour cream into the soup and cook until the cheese has melted, without letting it come to a boil.
11. Season with salt and pepper and serve garnished with the potato skins and the remaining bacon, cheese, green onions and sour cream.

Nutrition Facts: Calories 712, Fat 71g (Saturated 33g, Trans 1g), Cholesterol 166mg, Sodium 1220mg,
Carbs 55g (Fiber 4g, Sugars 9g), Protein 38g

Hungarian Mushroom Soup

Prep Time: 10 minutes **Cook Time**: 25 minutes
Total Time: 35 minutes **Servings**: 4

A Hungarian style mushroom soup seasoned with
paprika, dill and sour cream.

ingredients
2 tablespoons butter
1 onion, diced
1 pound mushrooms, sliced
1/4 cup flour (rice flour for gluten-free)
1 tablespoon paprika
4 cups vegetable broth (or chicken broth)
2 teaspoons dried dill
1 tablespoon soy sauce (optional)
1/2 cup sour cream
1 tablespoon lemon juice (optional)
salt and pepper to taste
1 handful fresh dill, chopped (optional)

directions
1. Melt the butter in a large saucepan over medium
   heat, add the onion and mushrooms and cook
   until the mushrooms have released their liquids
   and it has evaporated, about 10-15 minutes.
2. Mix in the flour and paprika and let it cook for 2-3 minutes.
3. Add the broth, dill, soy sauce, bring to a boil, reduce the heat and simmer for 10 minutes
4. Add the sour cream and lemon juice, and season with salt and pepper before adding the dill.

Slow Cooker: Implement step 1 and 2, place everything except the sour cream, lemon and dill in the slow
cooker and cook on low for 6-10 hours or high for 2-4 hours before adding the sour cream, lemon and
dill.

Nutrition Facts: Calories 209, Fat 12g (Saturated 7g, Trans 0), Cholesterol 30mg, Sodium 498mg,
Carbs 17g (Fiber 2g, Sugars 5g), Protein 10g

Split Pea Soup with Ham Hock

Prep Time: 15 minutes **Cook Time**: 1 hour 45 minutes
Total Time: 2 hours **Servings**: 4

A split pea soup that is slowly simmered with a smoky ham hock; winter comfort food couldn't get any simpler or tastier than this!

ingredients
1 tablespoon oil
1 onion, diced
2 carrots, diced
2 stalks celery, diced
2 cloves garlic, chopped
1 teaspoon thyme, chopped
6 cups ham stock (or chicken broth or water)
1 pound split peas, picked over
1 ham hock
2 bay leaves
cayenne, salt, and pepper to taste

directions
1. Heat the oil in a large saucepan over medium heat, add the onions, carrots and celery and cook until tender, about 10-15 minutes.
2. Add the garlic and thyme and cook until fragrant, about a minute.
3. Add the broth, split peas, ham hock and bay leaves, bring to a boil, reduce the heat and simmer, covered, until the spit peas are soft, about 1-2 hours.
4. Remove the ham hock and bay leaves, season with cayenne , salt, and pepper to taste and mash or puree with a hand blender to desired consistency.
5. Shred the meat from the ham hock, return to soup and either enjoy immediately or let simmer on low for a few more hours to bring out more flavour.

Option: Garnish with sour cream.
Option: Garnish with grainy mustard.

Nutrition Facts: Calories 797, Fat 20g (Saturated 5g, Trans 0), Cholesterol 79mg, Sodium 1606mg, Carbs 93g (Fiber 31g, Sugars 17g), Protein 61g

Sweet Potato, Black Bean and Chorizo Soup

Prep Time: 10 minutes **Cook Time**: 50 minutes
Total Time: 1 hour **Servings**: 4

A sweet potato and black bean soup with spicy chorizo sausage that's bound to warm you up on a cold winter day!

ingredients

1/2 pound chorizo sausage, casings removed
1 tablespoon olive oil
1 onion, diced
2 cloves garlic, chopped
1 teaspoon ground cumin
1 pinch ground cinnamon (optional)
4 cups chicken broth (or vegetable broth)
1 large sweet potato, peeled and cut into bite sized
　　pieces
2 (14.5 ounce) cans black beans
1 (14.5 ounce) can diced tomatoes
2 chipotle chilies in adobo, chopped
salt and pepper to taste
1 tablespoon lime juice
2 tablespoons cilantro, chopped

directions

1. Cook the chorizo in a large saucepan over medium-high heat, breaking it apart as it cooks, about 8-10 minutes, and set aside.
2. Add the oil, if required, and the onion, and cook until tender, about 5-7 minutes.
3. Add the garlic, cumin and cinnamon and cook until fragrant, about a minute.
4. Add the broth, sweet potato, black beans, diced tomatoes and chipotles, bring to a boil, reduce the heat and simmer until the sweet potatoes are tender, about 15-20 minutes.
5. Puree 1/3 of the soup, add the chorizo and simmer for another 10 minutes.
6. Season with salt and pepper, mix in the lime juice and cilantro.

Option: Omit the sausage for vegetarian.
Option: Garnish with your favourites such as: avocado, sour cream, cheese, etc..

Nutrition Facts: Calories 465, Fat 18g (Saturated 5g, Trans 0), Cholesterol 39mg, Sodium 1204mg, Carbs 53g (Fiber 19g, Sugars 8g), Protein 23g

Pasta e Fagioli Soup (Italian Pasta and Bean Soup)

Prep Time: 10 minutes **Cook Time**: 50 minutes
Total Time: 1 hour **Servings**: 4

A tasty Italian style bean and pasta soup with Italian sausage and plenty of vegetables.

ingredients
1/2 pound Italian sausage, casings removed
1 tablespoon olive oil
1 onion, diced
2 carrots, diced
2 stalks celery, diced
3 cloves garlic, chopped
1 pinch red pepper flakes (optional)
1/2 teaspoon ground fennel seeds (optional)
1 tablespoon tomato paste
1/4 cup white wine (or broth)
4 cups ham broth (or chicken broth)
1 (14.5 ounce) can diced tomatoes
2 (14.5 ounce) cans cannellini beans
1 teaspoon oregano
1 bay leaf
1 (2 inch) piece parmigiano reggiano (parmesan)
   rind (optional)
1 cup ditalini pasta (gluten-free for gluten-free)
salt and pepper to taste
1 tablespoon parsley, chopped (optional)

directions
1. Cook the sausage in a large saucepan over medium-high heat and set aside.
2. Add the oil, onion, carrots and celery to the pan and cook until tender, about 10-15 minutes.
3. Add the garlic, red pepper flakes, fennel seeds, and tomato paste, and cook until fragrant, about a minute.
4. Add the wine and deglaze the pan.
5. Add the broth, sausage, tomatoes, beans, oregano, bay leaf and parmesan rind, bring to a boil, reduce the heat and simmer for 15 minutes.
6. Add the pasta and simmer until it is cooked al-dente, about 6-8 minutes.
7. Season with salt and pepper and serve garnished with parsley and parmesan.

Slow Cooker: Implement step 1, optionally implement steps 2-4, place everything except the beans and pasta in the slow cooker and cook on low for 6-10 hours or high for 2-4 hours before adding the beans and pasta and cooking on high until the pasta is al dente, about 20-30 minutes.

Nutrition Facts: Calories 661, Fat 24g (Saturated 8g, Trans 0), Cholesterol 47mg, Sodium 609mg, Carbs 78g (Fiber 15g, Sugars 7g), Protein 31g

Shrimp Bisque

Prep Time: 15 minutes **Cook Time**: 1 hour 25 minutes
Total Time: 1 hour 40 minutes **Servings**: 4

A decadently smooth and creamy shrimp bisque
filled with chunks of succulent shrimp.

ingredients
1 pound shrimp, peeled, deveined, roughly chopped,
    shells reserved
1 tablespoon oil
1 tablespoon butter
1 cup onion, diced
2 carrots, diced
2 stalks celery, diced
2 cloves garlic, chopped
2 tablespoons flour (or rice flour for gluten-free)
2 cups shrimp stock (or chicken broth or dashi)
2 cups water
1 (14.5 ounce) can tomatoes, crushed
1/4 cup dry sherry
2 tablespoons brandy
1 sprig thyme
1 bay leaf
1/4 cup arborio rice
2 tablespoons tomato paste
1 tablespoon paprika
1 tablespoon butter
2 tablespoons dry white wine
1/4 cup dry sherry
2 tablespoons brandy
2/3 cup heavy cream
salt and pepper to taste
1/2 lemon, juice

directions
1. Heat the oil and melt the butter in a large sauce pan over medium heat, add the onion, carrots
   and celery and cook until tender, about 10-15 minutes.
2. Add the garlic and shrimp shells and cook for 2 minutes.
3. Mix in the flour and cook for 2-3 minutes.
4. Add the stock, water, tomatoes, sherry, brandy, thyme and bay leaf, bring to a boil, reduce the
   heat and simmer, covered, for 30 minutes.
5. Strain the liquid into another saucepan and discard the solids.
6. Add the rice, tomato paste and paprika, bring to a boil, reduce the heat and simmer, covered,
   until the rice is cooked, about 20-30 minutes.
7. Melt the butter in a pan over medium heat, add the shrimp, and cook until just cooked, about
   2-3 minutes per side.
8. Add the wine and deglaze the pan.
9. Add half of the shrimp and the juices to the soup and puree until smooth with an immersion
   blender or in a food processor or blender.

10. Add the remaining shrimp, sherry, brandy and cream and heat to serve.
11. Season with salt, pepper and lemon juice.

Nutrition Facts: Calories 497, Fat 25g (Saturated 13g, Trans 0.3g), Cholesterol 252mg, Sodium 383mg, Carbs 30g (Fiber 5g, Sugars 8g), Protein 27g

Pot Roast Mushroom Soup

Prep Time: 10 minutes **Cook Time**: 40 minutes
Total Time: 50 minutes **Servings**: 4

Got some leftover pot roast? You can't go wrong using it in this rich and flavourful pot roast soup with mushrooms!

ingredients
3 tablespoons butter
1 small onion, diced
2 cloves garlic, chopped
1 teaspoon thyme, chopped
8 ounces mushrooms, sliced
1/4 cup flour (or rice flour for gluten-free)
1/4 cup red wine
4 cups beef broth
2 cups pot roast, cooked and shredded
1 tablespoon parsley, chopped

directions
1. Melt the butter in a large saucepan over medium heat, add the onion and mushrooms and cook until the mushrooms have released their moisture and it has evaporated, about 15-20 minutes.
2. Add the garlic and thyme and cook until fragrant, about 1 minute.
3. Mix in the flour and cook for 2-3 minutes.
4. Add the wine and deglaze the pan.
5. Add the broth and beef, bring to a boil, reduce the heat and simmer for 15 minutes.
6. Mix in the parsley and enjoy!

Nutrition Facts: Calories 171, Fat 9g (Saturated 5g, Trans 0.3g), Cholesterol 22mg, Sodium 481mg, Carbs 13g (Fiber 1g, Sugars 3g), Protein 7g

White Chicken Chili Soup

Prep Time: 10 minutes **Cook Time**: 20 minutes
Total Time: 30 minutes **Servings**: 4

A tasty white chicken chili with beans.

ingredients
1 tablespoon oil
1 onion, diced
2 jalapeno peppers, sliced
2 cloves garlic, chopped
1 tablespoon ground cumin
4 cups chicken broth (or chicken stock)
2 cups chicken, cooked and shredded
2 (14.5 ounce) cans white beans, drained and rinsed
2 (4.5 ounce) cans chopped green chilies
1 teaspoon oregano
2 tablespoon masa or cornmeal (optional)
1/2 cup heavy cream (or milk)
2 tablespoons cilantro, chopped (optional)
salt and pepper to taste

directions
1. Heat the oil in a pan over medium heat, add the onion and jalapenos, and cook until tender, about 5-7 minutes.
2. Add the garlic and cumin, and cook until fragrant, about a minute.
3. Add the chicken broth, chicken, white beans, green chilies, oregano, and masa, bring to a boil, reduce the heat and simmer for 10 minutes.
4. Turn off the heat, mix in the cream, and cilantro, and season with salt and pepper to taste

Option: Serve garnished with your favourite taco toppings such as avocado, sour cream, cheese, etc.

Nutrition Facts: Calories 578, Fat 19g (Saturated 4g, Trans 0), Cholesterol 62mg, Sodium 674mg, Carbs 65g (Fiber 12g, Sugars 7g), Protein 37g

About Nutrition Facts

The nutritional facts were calculated using automated tools and they should be considered to be estimates. If you have any dietary requirements based on the nutrition facts you should calculate them yourself using a trusted source, using the nutrition facts of the ingredients and brands of products that you use in the recipes.

Other Cookbooks by Closet Cooking

Game Day Party Food

Melty Grilled Cheese

The Best of Closet Cooking 2012

The Best of Closet Cooking 2013

More Recipes

If you liked these recipes, you can find more on ClosetCooking.com

Printed in Great Britain
by Amazon

35328935R00025